The Little Book of Garlic

Alastair Williams

Summersdale Publishers Ltd
46 West Street
Chichester
West Sussex
PO19 1RP
UK

www.summersdale.com

Printed and bound in Great Britain

ISBN 1 84024 386 4

With additional text by Susie Jones.

Contents

Introduction

Without garlic I simply would not care to live.
— Louis Diat (1885–1958)

Surely no herb inspires more love – or loathing – than garlic. With its pungent flavour and indisputable medicinal properties, the 'stinking rose' has a long and illustrious history as both culinary ingredient and popular heal-all.

Incredibly versatile in the kitchen, garlic makes an indispensable contribution to a huge number of national cuisines; Indian, Chinese and French to name but a few. Long shunned by English cooks, garlic's popularity in recent decades has risen to such heights that it is now considered an essential store cupboard item. Its mouth-watering flavours range from the richly mellow of roast garlic to the sharp zing of raw, adding pizzazz and style to the most mundane of dishes. But it's not just in the kitchen that garlic shines.

Aside from its noted vampire-repelling properties, garlic has long been valued for its ability to alleviate and cure many different ailments, from high blood pressure, to the common cold, to bee stings. It is antibiotic, antiseptic and acts as an antioxidant – no wonder the old folk rhyme:

Eat onions in March and garlic in May,
Then the rest of the year, your doctor can play.

So whether you want to grow your own garlic, experiment with some of the amazing home remedies that can be made from garlic, or simply want to expand your repertoire of fabulous garlic-based creations, this book has it all: garlic ice cream for the adventurous, garlic soup for the sick, and garlic olives for the gourmet! Enjoy.

The History of
Garlic

A member of the lily family, garlic originated in central Asia. The bulb spread all over the world, as did knowledge of its healing properties. The widespread use of garlic in the ancient world is well documented: cuneiform tablets dating back to 3000 BC show that the Assyrians used garlic to ease swollen joints and fight infections; ancient Chinese records list the uses of garlic in both cookery and medicine as early as 2000 BC; and garlic is cited as a medical panacea by the famous second century AD Greek physician Galen.

The historian Herodotus records in his *Histories* that on the great pyramid of Cheops, which was constructed around 2680 BC:

There is an inscription in Egyptian characters on the pyramid which records the quantity of radishes, onions and garlic consumed by the labourers who constructed it; and I perfectly well remember that the interpreter who read the writing to me said that the money expended in this way was 1600 talents of silver.

Garlic was considered to be such an essential part of the diet of labourers working on the pyramids that strikes ensued when the garlic ration was cut. The importance ascribed to garlic in ancient Egyptian culture can be inferred from the fact that Egyptians swore oaths by it and used it to keep evil spirits from tombs, including the most famous tomb of all, that of Tutankhamun. Small bulbs of garlic were found sealed in his tomb along with the excesses of gold and precious gems – truly 'wonderful things!'

Perhaps the most famous literary reference to garlic, and the one that established garlic as the darling of the doctors throughout the civilised world, is in Homer's *Odyssey*. Hermes advises Odysseus to eat the plant *moly*, or golden garlic, in order to protect him from being turned into a pig by the sorceress Circe:

'Take this herb, which is one of great virtue, and keep it about you when you go to Circe's house, it will be a talisman to you against every kind of mischief.

'And I will tell you of all the wicked witchcraft that Circe will try to practise upon you. She will mix a mess for you to drink, and she will drug the meal with which she makes it, but she will not be able to charm you, for the virtue of the herb that I shall give you will prevent her spells from working.' [...]

As he spoke he pulled the herb out of the ground and showed me what it was like. The root was black, while the flower was as white as milk; the gods call it Moly, and mortal men cannot uproot it, but the gods can do whatever they like.

Garlic was gradually dispersed throughout Europe by travellers passing through the region. It was brought to Britain by the Romans, but the word 'garlic' itself is thought to originate from the Anglo-Saxon 'gar', meaning spear, and 'leac', meaning leek. Garlic (*allium sativum*) and leek (*allium porrum*) are of the same family, but there is some disagreement over whether 'gar' relates to the shape of the leaves or the thrusting nature of the leaves themselves.

Although mentioned by Chaucer, garlic was not actually cultivated in English gardens until around 1540. However, its cultivation must not be taken to mean that garlic had stunk its way out of the stigma of being slave fodder and was to be admitted into the kitchen. Whilst on the continent Henry IV of France chewed garlic whenever he could, and was reputed to have 'a breath that could fell an ox at twenty paces', by the reign of Queen Elizabeth I garlic was considered taboo in English court circles, fit only for consumption by the lower orders. Two English texts from the seventeenth century, Nicholas Culpeper's *Culpeper's Complete Herbal* and John Evelyn's *Acetaria: A Discourse of Sallats*, make it obvious that whilst garlic was accepted and employed as a useful and freely available cure-all, it was not for the English palate. Evelyn wrote:

Garlick, Allium; dry towards Excess; and tho' both by Spaniards and Italians, and the more Southern People, familiarly eaten, with almost everything, and esteem'd of such singular Vertue to help Concoction, and thought a Charm against all Infection and Poyson (by which it has obtain'd the Name of the Country man's Theriacle) ... we absolutely forbid it entrance into our Salleting [salad], by reason of its intolerable Rankness, and which made it so detested of old, that the eating of it was ... part of the Punishment of such as had committed the horrid'st Crimes. To be sure, 'tis not for Ladies' Palats, nor those who court them, farther than to permit a light touch on the Dish, with a Clove thereof.

> *It provokes urine, and women's courses, helps the biting of mad dogs and other venomous creatures, kills worms in children, cuts and voids tough phlegm, purges the head, helps the lethargy, is a good preservative against, and a remedy for, any plague, sore or foul ulcers; takes away spots and blemishes in the skin, eases pains in the ears, ripens and breaks imposthumes, or other swellings.*
>
> — Nicholas Culpeper,
> *Culpeper's Complete Herbal*

British disdain for clove consumption persisted until very recently. The population of countries such as Spain and France may consume on average 50 g of garlic per day, but in Britain extra garlic was grown in the two world wars not to eat, but to use to treat wounds. Even now, as recently as 2000, the Queen caused a furore when she insisted that Italian chefs exclude garlic from the menu on her state visit to Italy. Although royal reason prevailed in deciding to exclude garlic from a busy schedule of breathing over important people, British society as a whole was unwilling to accept the bulb, social engagements or no. The bland, boiled, 'meat and two veg' mentality was highly resistant to what was essentially a foreign herb, and the disdain for garlic and 'garlic eaters' is evident in British attitudes over the centuries. Percy Bysshe Shelley, writing home during a visit to Italy in 1818, wrote:

What do you think? Young women of rank eat — you will never guess what — garlick! Our poor friend Lord Byron is quite corrupted by living among these people, and in fact, is going on in a way not worthy of him.

It is only recently that garlic has become a regular feature in British cooking, largely due to a more open-minded approach, a wider availability of ingredients, and the converging threads of garlic's benefits to both health and cuisine. Garlic is now more or less indispensable to a whole range of dishes, many of which are featured in this book, although it is fair to say that none can hold to be traditionally British.

> *Eat not garlic nor onions, lest they find out thy boorish origin by the smell.*
> — Cervantes, *Don Quixote*

Garlic in Folklore
and Religion

As one of the oldest and most widely used herbs, it is unsurprising that garlic features in everything from religious texts to creation myths to age-old superstitions. Garlic's distinctive taste, strong smell and almost magical healing properties gave the bulb an aura of mystery that was most easily explained through story and myth.

In Islam, it is said that when Satan left the Garden of Eden, garlic sprouted from where he planted his left foot. This accounts for its unpleasant odour, an attribute that prompted the prophet Muhammad to ban believers from entering a mosque after having eaten garlic. Similarly, in Hindu myth when the god Vishnu slices the head off Rahu, the demon that causes eclipses, foul-smelling garlic sprouts from the putrid blood seeping from Rahu's neck.

> *Common names: garlic, allium, stinking rose, rustic treacle, nectar of the gods, camphor of the poor, poor man's treacle, stinkweed, ajo, Russian penicillin*

In Roman times garlic's fiery taste and ability to furnish the consumer with fighting strength and spirit meant that it was associated with Mars, the Roman god of war. The ancient Greeks, however, linked garlic with Hecate, the triple goddess who represented maiden, mother and crone. Hecate inhabited the Underworld and had power over birth, life and death, powers reflected in the almost miraculous healing abilities of garlic.

> *Always take a bite of onion before speeding forth to battle, just as your patrons of the cock-pit give their birds a feed of garlic before they put them for the fight.*
>
> — Xenophon, *The Symposium*

Perhaps one of the best known myths relating to garlic, however, is the belief in its power to ward off vampires. In Bram Stoker's *Dracula*, the connection that Stoker makes between Dracula, the forces of evil and the Evil Eye, and the ability of garlic to protect against all three, was merely a case of him tapping into popularly held European beliefs. It evidently took a powerfully scented plant to ward off such a powerfully evil creature as a vampire, for amongst the arsenal of anti-vampire measures such as the Christian crucifixes and holy water, more natural, traditional charms such as sunlight, running water, and, of course, garlic were included.

On the eves of the feasts of St George and St Andrew, it was felt necessary not only to stay inside with a light burning throughout the night, but also to rub excessive amounts of garlic round doorways and windows to bar the entrance of vampires. Livestock that were forced to take a chance and stay outside were not forgotten – they too were smeared with garlic. In Eastern Europe the presence of vampires was believed to account for the plague in a village, leading those born out of wedlock or unbaptised to leave instructions for 'necessary precautions' in their will to prevent them from rising again, undead. These included driving a stake through their heart, cutting off their head, and, naturally, stuffing their mouth with garlic.

We went into the room, taking the flowers with us. The Professor's actions were certainly odd and not to be found in any pharmacopeia that I ever heard of. First he fastened up the windows and latched them securely. Next, taking a handful of the flowers, he rubbed them all over the sashes, as though to ensure that every whiff of air that might get in would be laden with the garlic smell. Then with the wisp he rubbed all over the jamb of the door, above, below, and at each side, and round the fireplace in the same way. It all seemed grotesque to me, and presently I said, 'Well, Professor, I know you always have a reason for what you do, but this certainly puzzles me. It is well we have no sceptic here, or he would say that you were working some spell to keep out an evil spirit.'

> *'Perhaps I am!' He answered quietly as he began to make the wreath which Lucy was to wear round her neck.*
>
> — Bram Stoker, *Dracula*

In Greece, garlic is believed to keep away evil spirits and devils, as these beings fear the bulb. Traditionally Greeks carried it in their garments or hung it in their homes to keep away these malevolent forces and also to protect from the Evil Eye, while in Spain bullfighters carry garlic to protect themselves from the bull's charge.

> *If ever any man with impious hand strangle an aged parent, may he eat garlic, deadlier than the hemlock!*
>
> — Horace, *Epodes III*

Koreans used to consume pickled garlic for protection against the danger of marauding tigers whenever they had to travel through mountain passes. This belief had its origins in the birth story of Tangun, the creation myth of the Korean nation. A tiger and a bear come to Hwan-Woong, son of the king who rules the heavens, and beg to be turned into humans. They are sent into a cave to survive on nothing but garlic and prayer for twenty days. The tiger cannot take the restrictive diet and constant confinement and flees, whilst the bear continues and is turned into the first woman as a reward for his efforts and endurance.

The protective powers of garlic mean that it symbolises security and practicality. Dreaming of garlic has therefore been interpreted as a sign that the dreamer is searching for security in love, and that they will listen to their head rather than their heart. A dream of wandering through a garlic patch signifies to a young woman that she will marry for practicality rather than love, and to others that they will excel in their chosen field.

Garlic's place in religion is not only dependent on its ability to protect, but also concerns itself with celebrating the gift of this basic food, even if it was more of a bane than a blessing for the poor Korean tiger. During Noruz, the Iranian New Year, a table is laid with the *haft-seen*, Persian for the Seven 'S's. These echo the seven *Amesha Spentas* or Bounteous Immortals of Zoroastrianism, and are usually a combination of various foodstuffs, one of which is *seer* – garlic. Other religions, however, hold that you can have too much of a good thing: while revering garlic for its medicinal properties, Hare Krishnas do not eat it as they believe it 'strongly increase[s] the mode of passion, which leads to loss of concentration, patience and tolerance'.

The rabble who had joined the people were overcome by greed, and the Sons of Israel began to wail again, 'Who will give us meat to eat?' they said. 'Think of the fish we used to eat free in Egypt, the cucumbers, melons, leeks, onions and garlic! Here we are, wasting away, stripped of everything: there is nothing but manna for us to look at.'

– The Bible, Numbers 11: 4-6

Growing Garlic

There are two main types of garlic:

Softneck (allium sativum var. sativum)

This is the variety most commonly found in supermarkets as it keeps for longer and is easier to grow. It has white, papery skin, a large number of cloves and a flexible stalk. There are two main varieties of softneck garlic – artichoke and silverskin. The silverskin is more common as it is easier to grow, while the artichoke has a milder flavour.

Hardneck (allium sativum var. ophioscorodon)

This variety has a stalk that emerges from the top of the cloves to produce clusters of bubils, sometimes called garlic flowers. It is generally harder to grow than softneck garlic and does not keep so well due to the thin nature of the protective outer skin. The cloves are, however, larger, fewer in number and have a better flavour. The three main varieties of hardneck garlic are rocambole, porcelain and purple stripe. Rocambole has brownish cloves, porcelain garlic is very white and has a few huge cloves, and purple stripe's distinguishing feature is, well, fairly self-explanatory.

If you can spare the space and don't mind the appearance, garlic makes an excellent container plant. Water regularly and use plenty of compost and the plants will be more than happy!

It is possible to grow any of these five sorts of garlic, although some may be more suited to certain types of soil and climatic conditions than others. Silverskins, porcelains and purple stripes, whilst hardier than rocamboles, do not tolerate hot, dry springs, although artichokes are likely to survive almost anywhere. All in all it is reckoned that there are now over 450 different varieties of garlic for you to choose from.

Recent research has given an age-old piece of gardening lore new credence. A study made by a biologist from Newcastle University showed that garlic provides a very effective antidote to the unwanted attentions of slugs and snails. Its heady aroma not only repels them, but also actually causes them to shrivel and die within a matter of hours. This trick was popular in monastery gardens in the Middle Ages, when monks used to shield precious plants by planting a wall of garlic round them.

Top Garlic Growing Tips

Choose the patch of your garden that gets most sun to allow the bulbs to ripen.

Where you live depends upon when you plant your garlic. In the United Kingdom, it is recommended that you plant in October as this generally produces the biggest, ripest cloves. Spring planting does not guarantee this and is best left to warmer climes.

If planting in October, however, hardier garlic than the average supermarket variety is required. Although it is possible to grow supermarket garlic, it can be haphazard, and a trip to the garden centre might be necessary in order to invest in a hardier variety, such as the artichoke.

Make sure the bed is well drained to avoid the bulbs rotting over the winter. Add as much organic matter as possible when digging the top 15 cm of soil in your intended bed, and if possible some sand to aid drainage.

Separate the cloves of the bulb and select the biggest, juiciest looking specimens. Place them in an upright position just below the surface in your prepared bed at 10 cm intervals.

Look after your garlic. Water it if necessary, keep it weed free and try to feed it twice a month. Garlic is generally pest and disease free, but can be prone to suffer from similar problems as the onion, such as white and neck rot, or visits from the onion fly. Watch for early signs of these problems and they should be easily treatable.

By mid-August, the garlic is ready to harvest. The green shoots that should have appeared in the spring will have turned a yellowish-brown colour. If left any longer they are in danger of resprouting and are less likely to keep. Ease them out gently to avoid breaking up the cloves and eat before they dry out when they are at their sweetest.

Garlic features strongly in the list of companion plants for gardeners. If planted around roses it can cure black spot. It is also said to protect against powdery mildew in roses and carrots.

Garlic Recipes

Garlic Soup

Garlic soup saves lives

— Provençal saying

Ingredients
  1 tbsp olive oil
  at least 20 cloves of garlic, peeled and thinly sliced
  1 large white onion, diced
  2 leeks, diced
  1 tsp fresh rosemary
  16 fl oz vegetable or chicken stock
  3 fl oz dry sherry
  cayenne pepper to taste
  1 tbsp fresh basil, shredded
  salt to taste
  lemon juice to taste

Method

Heat the oil in a saucepan on a low heat. Add the garlic, leek and onions. Sauté, covered, for about 25 minutes until soft and colourless. Blend in a food processor with the rosemary and a quarter of the stock.

Pour mixture back in saucepan and add remaining stock and sherry. Simmer for 20 minutes. Stir in cayenne and fresh basil. Add salt and lemon juice to taste, and serve immediately.

> *If you wish to take away the smell of garlic on your breath, then simply chew some parsley.*

Garlic Bread

A terribly easy version of the family favourite, and immensely satisfying if you resent having to pay for ready-made garlic bread. For an exciting alternative add grated mozzarella cheese mixed with boulders of garlic after the underside has been toasted, and grill until the cheese melts.

Ingredients
1 French loaf or similar
4 tsp butter
4 tsp finely chopped fresh garlic – more if desired
1 tbsp Italian seasoning
1 tbsp oregano

Method

Slice the bread in half and then again lengthways. Give each of the four halves a few deep cuts to allow the bread to be ultra-absorbent. Mix the garlic and butter together in a bowl to form a creamy garlic butter.

Spread the mixture evenly over the bread, making sure the slits on each slice are deeply filled.

Place under a pre-heated medium-high grill, butter side down, until golden brown.

Turn over and repeat.

Serve immediately.

Garlic Ice Cream

Don't knock it until you've tried it! A must for all serious garlic lovers and a regular feature of most garlic festivals. Try it with a chilli 'flake'.

Ingredients

- 16 fl oz whole milk
- 3 cloves of garlic, diced
- 1 vanilla pod, split in half
- 8 fl oz double cream
- 12 oz granulated sugar
- 9 egg yolks

Method

Combine vanilla, milk and garlic in a pan. Bring to the boil, then remove from heat and set aside. Cream together egg yolks, sugar and cream in large bowl.

Strain the milky mixture into the egg and sugar cream, stirring all the while.

Return to the pan in its entirety and stir continuously over medium heat until it is thick enough to coat the back of a spoon. This should take about 10–15 minutes.

Cool down in an ice bath, then freeze until firm.

Garlic Olives

A wonderful way to dress up ordinary olives. Presented in an attractive jar they can also make an inexpensive Christmas present for the connoisseur.

Ingredients
  3 oz pitted green olives
  3 oz pitted black olives
  3 garlic cloves
  3 very thin slices of lemon
  1 tsp black peppercorns
  3 bay leaves
  whole sprigs dried thyme, basil and oregano
  2 fl oz sherry or vinegar
  olive oil

Method

Combine all ingredients in an airtight container, preferably an attractive jar. Cover with olive oil and leave to marinate, at least overnight.

> *After handling garlic, scrub your hands with salt, lemon juice and cold water. Follow this with a dip in warm, soapy water for odour-free fingers! Rubbing your hands over stainless steel can also help to cover your garlicky tracks.*

Garlic Power Potion

A must as soon as the inevitable winter cold or fever rears its ugly head. This drink is packed with vitamin C and vital trace elements, but is not for the faint hearted. If it packs too much of a kick, try stirring in a teaspoon of honey.

Ingredients
3 crushed garlic cloves
dash of Ribena to taste
juice of 1 lemon
sprinkling of cayenne pepper
water

Method

Place garlic and Ribena in bottom of large mug.
Top up with boiling water.
  Add lemon juice and cayenne pepper. Stir.
  Wait until a suitable temperature and sip whilst
hunched in favourite chair.

> *When chopping garlic, smash it against a
> chopping board with the flat side of a large knife.
> The cloves will be far easier to peel. Sprinkling
> salt on the garlic will also stop it from sticking
> to the knife during chopping.*

Garlic Bloody Mary

How has this classic drink survived for so long without the addition of garlic? If the slightly 'bitty' texture is offensive, then simply blend until smooth, a method that allows for the addition of tinned tomatoes if no tomato juice is available. For an exciting alternative, why not use this as a base for soups, chilli and pasta sauces?

Ingredients
   1.5 fl oz vodka
   3 fl oz tomato sauce
   2–3 drops Tabasco Sauce
   7 drops Worcestershire Sauce

3 garlic cloves, minced
Dash of lemon juice to taste
Pepper
Salt
Garlic salt
Celery salt

Method

Combine ingredients. Pour over crushed ice.

Garlic cooks faster than onions. If instructed to sauté garlic and onions together, bear in mind that the garlic will lose its flavour if cooked for too long. For a more flavoursome meal, add the garlic later when the onions are almost soft.

When choosing garlic heads at the supermarket, always select bulbs that are firm when pressed. Avoid sprouting garlic, which has been around for longer. Once purchased, keep for two or three weeks, but do not refrigerate.

Cod wants garlic
– Brazilian saying

Garlic boiled, garlic lost
 – Spanish proverb

Each garlic clove contains 5 calories, 0 g of fat, and provides 2 per cent of your Recommended Daily Allowance of vitamin C

Wel loved he garleek, onyons and eek leekers,
And for to drinken strong wyn, reed as blood.
— Chaucer, *The Canterbury Tales*

What garlic is to salad, insanity is to art.
— Augustus Saint-Gaudens, *Reminiscences*

But if, out of humour, and hungry, alone
A man should sit down to dinner, each one
Of the dishes which the cook chooses to spoil
With a horrible mixture of garlic and oil,
The chances are ten against one, I must own,
He gets up as ill-tempered as when he sat down.
– Edward Robert Bulwer Lytton, *Lucile*

A garlic caress is stimulating.
A garlic excess soporific.
– Curnonsky (1872-1956)

Garlic for Health

> *Garlics, tho' used by the French are better adapted to the uses of medicine than cookery*
> – Amelia Simmons, *American Cookery*, 1796

Garlic has long been considered a miracle cure. It was commonly known as 'poor man's treacle', being freely available and used for such afflictions as might beset the average poor man. These included the need to neutralise animal poisons, an idea that survives in the notion that cut garlic rubbed against a bee sting alleviates the pain. According to Nicholas Culpeper, the seventeenth-century herbalist, garlic also worked against bites from mad dogs! Although this is perhaps not such an issue in today's world of strict quarantine laws, the swing towards alternative and natural medicines has secured garlic an unprecedented amount of attention. Odourless garlic is now available to encourage the more nasally sensitive to benefit from its properties, and a plethora of research has tried to quantify what our ancestors knew all along: garlic is good for you!

> *But I was more beholding to the Guianians than any other; for Antonio de Berreo told me that he could never attain to the knowledge thereof, and yet they taught me the best way of healing as well thereof as of all other poisons. Some of the Spaniards have been cured in ordinary wounds of the common poisoned arrows with the juice of garlic.*
>
> — Sir Walter Raleigh, in his account of the discovery of Guiana in 1595

The general principle to remember with garlic is that it is better for you raw. The fact that its potency decreases over time and is almost eradicated by cooking, as is its smell, has caused concern over the allicin content and therefore effectiveness of the new breed of odourless garlic. Allicin and its derivatives are the main chemicals that are beneficial to the human body, produced whenever garlic begins to degrade through chopping or crushing. A powerful antibiotic and antifungal substance, allicin can therefore be used to treat basic skin and yeast infections.

A tried and tested way of doing this is to smear crushed garlic onto the affected areas, although it is worth adding a note of caution. The crushed garlic can be so vigorous that excessive contact provokes skin blistering. It is therefore wise to avoid this method for prolonged periods for time, and most especially for the treatment of yeast infections! In order to enjoy the other health goodies that allicin has to offer, including strengthening the immune system and limiting the growth of yeast in the first place, one might be better off seeking other methods. Consuming garlic is probably preferable to applying it liberally to the skin, although the addition of oil can help to dilute the pungent poultice.

Garlic is as good as ten mothers
— Indian proverb

Diallyl sulphides, transformation products of allicin, form another significant group of 'friendly' substances that are released whenever raw garlic gets a good beating. They survive cooking more successfully than allicin does, and, although they do not have allicin's antifungal properties, they have a host of other hidden bonuses. It is the diallyl sulphides that have chief responsibility for giving garlic its anticarcinogenic reputation. Simply eating garlic can guard against the risk of stomach cancer, and even inhibits the growth of tumours. They, along with other allicin products, also have a highly beneficial effect on the cardiovascular system, including lowering levels of harmful Low-Density Lipoprotein (LDL) cholesterol and guarding against blood clotting by unclogging arteries and regulating blood pressure.

> *In snowy weather, garlic is worth as much as a horse*
>
> – Spanish proverb

The general principle of many of these properties were noted long before modern research. The Roman writer Pliny the Elder was convinced garlic cured suspected tumours, promoted and improved circulation of the blood and, perhaps more controversially, also claimed that garlic was an aphrodisiac. Despite the fact that garlic may be one of the most unsociable foods around, and no self-respecting person would even consider eating it on a first date, it *is* a renowned aphrodisiac. This may be because in certain forms garlic can not only improve circulation but also stimulate the production of nitric oxide synthase (NOS), the enzyme primarily responsible for the mechanism of erection.

> *Our Rabbis taught Five things were said of garlic: It satiates, it keeps the body warm, it brightens up the face, it increases semen, and kills parasites in the bowels.*
> — The Talmud, Baba Kama 82a

As if to make up for getting you into the situation in the first place, garlic can be especially useful during pregnancy. Taking garlic whilst pregnant is not only thought to be fairly safe, but it also reduces the risk of pre-eclampsia and boosts the weight of the baby. However, be warned that because of the unsettling effect of garlic on the digestive system, garlic is held by some to be best avoided at this time. Following pregnancy it can also increase the odour of the milk, the amount consumed by the infant and the period spent feeding.

> *Raw garlic and pure wine make a shrewd man*
> *— Spanish proverb*

Garlic is not just beneficial for humans. If you feed hens with garlic they will produce bigger eggs, although it is important to stop feeding them garlic when they begin to lay or their eggs will have a distinct garlicky flavour. For those with more conventional pets, it has been noted that fleas dislike the taste of garlic. If your dog agrees to consume the clove, then not only will he hopefully be a flea-free zone but it will have the added bonus of sweetening his breath! This can also work for horses. Garlic capsules are also sold as a supplement to keep canine worms at bay.

That is not to say that garlic is beneficial for all creatures great and small. A recent study investigating the appetite of leeches found that those leeches placed on an arm smeared with garlic died within two and a half hours!

> DEMOSTHENES: Now, bolt down these cloves of garlic.
> SAUSAGE-SELLER: Pray, what for?
> DEMOSTHENES: Well primed with garlic, you will have greater mettle for the fight. But hurry, make haste rapidly!
>
> — Aristophanes, *Knights*

Top Garlic
Health Tips

Verrucas: tape a thin slice of garlic onto the verruca and replace every day. It should disappear within the week.

Athlete's foot: place cloves of garlic between the toes, or dab crushed garlic onto the affected areas.

Throat infections: gargle with a mixture of crushed garlic, a brew of babul tree bark and lemon juice.

Ulcers: dab a mixture of crushed garlic and yoghurt onto the ulcer and look for something to bite on when the initial sting hits.

Cancer, asthma, diabetes, excess phlegm, and other general health problems: chew one clove of garlic a day.

Eat ransoms [garlic] in May and all year thereafter physicians may play

— English proverb

Other titles from Summersdale

alastair williams

bestselling author of
Student Grub

man about
the kitchen

recipes for the reluctant chef

summersdale *cookery*

student

GRUB

Alastair Williams

summersdale *cookery*

student veggie

GRUB

Alastair Williams

summersdale *cookery*

Luke Cox

the

BBQ

& CAMPFIRE RECIPE BOOK

summersdale *cookery*

www.summersdale.com